Level 1 • Part 2

Integrated Chinese

中文听说读写
中文聽説讀寫

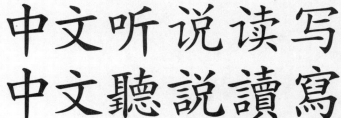

CHARACTER WORKBOOK
Simplified and Traditional Characters

Third Edition

THIRD EDITION BY

Yuehua Liu and Tao-chung Yao
Nyan-Ping Bi, Yaohua Shi, Liangyan Ge, Yea-fen Chen

ORIGINAL EDITION BY

Tao-chung Yao and Yuehua Liu
Yea-fen Chen, Liangyan Ge, Nyan-Ping Bi,
Xiaojun Wang, Yaohua Shi

CHENG & TSUI COMPANY
Boston

9th Printing, 2021

25 24 23 22 21   9 10 11 12 13

Published by
Cheng & Tsui Company, Inc.
25 West Street
Boston, MA 02111-1213 USA
Fax (617) 426-3669
www.cheng-tsui.com
"Bringing Asia to the World"™

ISBN 978-0-88727-676-7

Cover Design: studioradia.com

Cover Photographs: Man with map © Getty Images; Shanghai skyline © David Pedre/iStockphoto; Building with masks © Wu Jie; Night market © Andrew Buko. Used by permission.

Interior Design: hiSoft

The *Integrated Chinese* series includes books, workbooks, character workbooks, audio products, multimedia products, teacher's resources, and more. Visit **www.cheng-tsui.com** for more information on the other components of *Integrated Chinese*.

Printed in the United States of America

CONTENTS

Preface

This completely revised and redesigned Character Workbook is meant to accompany the third edition of *Integrated Chinese (IC)*. It has been over ten years since the *IC* series came into existence in 1997. During these years, amid all the historical changes that took place in China and the rest of the world, the demand for Chinese language teaching/learning materials has grown dramatically. We are greatly encouraged by the fact that *IC* not only has been a widely used textbook at the college level all over the United States and beyond, but also has become increasingly popular for advanced language students in high schools. Based on user feedback, we have made numerous changes so that the Character Workbook can become an even more useful tool for students of Chinese.

Stressing the importance of learning a new character by its components

Learning a new character becomes much easier if the student can identify its components. The student should learn how to write the 40 radicals at the beginning of the Character Workbook in the correct stroke order first, because these 40 radicals will appear repeatedly in other characters later. If a new character contains a component already familiar to the student, the stroke order of that component will not be introduced again. However, we will show the stroke order of all new components as they appear when we introduce new characters. For example, when we introduce the character 孩 (hái, child) in Lesson 2, we do not show the stroke order for the radical 子 (zǐ, son) because 子 already appeared in the radical section. Therefore, we only display the stroke order for the other component 亥 (hài, the last of the Twelve Earthly Branches). For the same reason, when 亥 appears in the new character 刻 (kè, quarter of an hour) in Lesson 3, its stroke order is not displayed. When the student learns a new character, he or she can easily tell if a component in the character has appeared in previous lessons. If the stroke order for that component is not displayed, it means that the component is not new. The student should try to recall where he or she has seen it before. By doing so, the student can connect new characters with old ones and build up a character bank. We believe that learning by association will help the student memorize characters better.

Main features of the new Character Workbook

a. Both traditional and simplified characters are introduced
If a character appears in both traditional and simplified forms, we show both to accommodate different learner needs.

b. Pinyin and English definition are clearly noted
We have moved the pinyin and the English definition above each character for easy recognition and review.

c. Radicals are highlighted

The radical of each character is highlighted. Knowing what radical group a character belongs to is essential when looking up that character in a traditional dictionary where the characters are arranged according to their radicals. To a certain extent, radicals can also help the student decipher the meaning of a character. For example, characters containing the radical 貝/贝 (bèi, shell), such as 貴/贵 (guì, expensive), and 貨/货 (huò, merchandise), are often associated with money or value. The student can group the characters sharing the same radical together and learn them by association.

d. Stroke order is prominently displayed

Another feature that we think is important is the numbering of each stroke in the order of its appearance. Each number is marked at the beginning of that particular stroke. We firmly believe that it is essential to write a character in the correct stroke order, and to know where each stroke begins and ends. To display the stroke order more prominently, we have moved the step-by-step character writing demonstration next to the main characters.

e. A "training wheel" is provided

We also provide grids with fine shaded lines inside to help the student better envision and balance their characters when practicing.

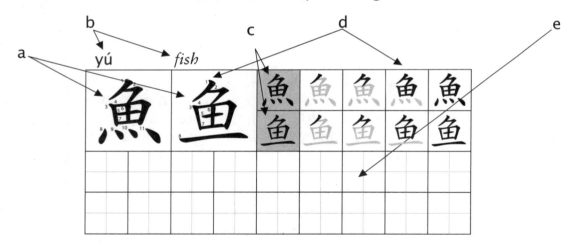

Other changes in the new edition

In order to focus on character recognition and acquisition, we decided not to include elements having to do with phonetic identification and phrase recognition.

To help the student look up characters more easily and to make the Character Workbook smaller and more portable, we decided to limit the indices to two, one arranged alphabetically by pinyin and the other by lesson. Additional appendices that are not directly linked to the practice of writing characters, such as the English-Chinese glossary, are available in the Textbook.

As in the textbook, low-frequency characters are indicated in gray in the Character Workbook.

The formation and radical of each character in this book are based on the *Modern Chinese Dictionary* (現代漢語詞典第五版／现代汉语词典第五版) published by the Commercial Press (商務印書館／商务印书馆). A total of 201 radicals and the stroke number and stroke order of each character all appear in that dictionary, and in some cases the same character is listed under more than one radical. For the characters in this book that fall in that category, we provide two radicals in order to facilitate students' dictionary searches. The two radicals are presented in order from top to bottom (e.g., 名: 夕, 口), left to right (e.g., 功：工, 力), and large to small (e.g., 章: 音, 立; 麻: 麻, 广). Also following the *Modern Chinese Dictionary*, we have made adjustments with regard to variant forms: For example, 嘴 and 滑 are presented as standard rather than 嘴 and 滑 respectively. Students, however, should be allowed to write the characters in their variant forms.

The changes that we made in the new version reflect the collective wishes of the users. We would like to take this opportunity to thank those who gave us feedback on how to improve the Character Workbook. We would like to acknowledge in particular Professor Hu Shuangbao of Beijing University, who read the entire manuscript and offered invaluable comments and suggestions for revision. Ms. Laurel Damashek at Cheng & Tsui assisted throughout the production process.

We hope you find this new edition useful. We welcome your comments and feedback. Please report any typos or other errors to **editor@cheng-tsui.com**.

Dialogue I

bǐ *to compare*

比 比 比 比 比 比

xuě *snow*

雪 雪 雪 雪 雪 雪

yuán *garden*

園 园 園 園 園 園 園 園 園 園 園
元 园 园 园 园

huá *slippery; to slide*

滑 滑 滑 滑 滑 滑 滑

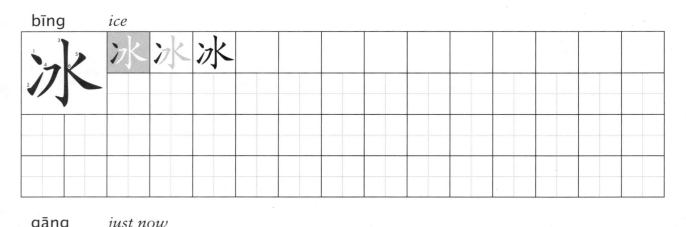

bīng *ice*

冰

冰 冰 冰

gāng *just now*

剛 刚

剛 剛 剛 剛 剛 剛 剛 剛 剛 剛
刚 刚 刚 刚 刚 刚

bào *newspaper; to report*

報 报

報 報 報 報 報 報 報 報 報 報
报 报 报 报 报 报

gèng *even more*

更

更 更 更 更 更 更

ér   *(conj.)*

而　而　而　而　而　而　而　而　而

qiě   *(conj.)*

且　且　且

nuǎn   *warm*

暖　暖　暖　暖　暖　暖　暖　暖

lěng   *cold*

冷　冷　冷　冷　冷　冷　冷

dié   *disc; small plate, dish, saucer*

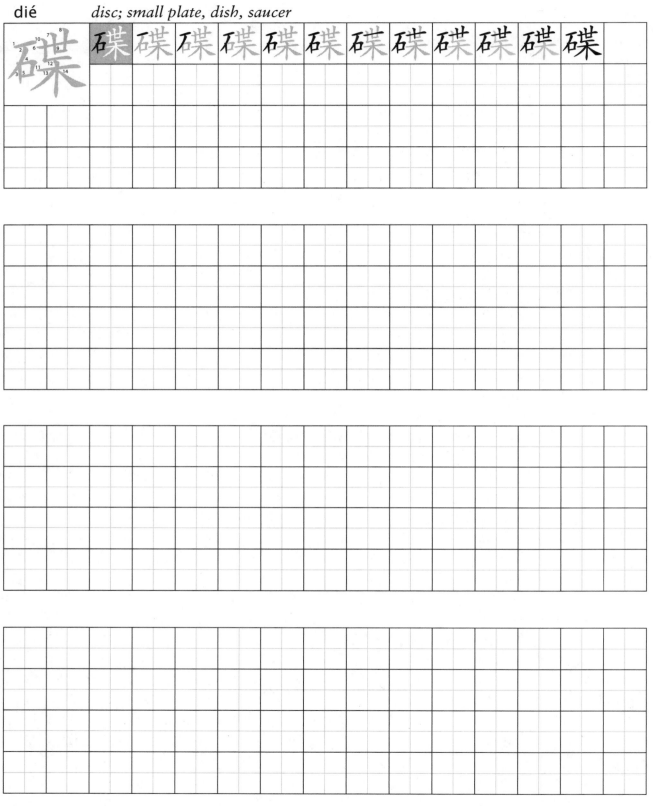

Dialogue II

fēi   *not, non-*

非 非 非 非 非 非 非 非 非 非 非

zāo   *rotten, decayed*

糟 糟 糟 糟 糟 糟 糟 糟 糟 糟

gāo   *cake*

糕 糕 糕 糕

dōng   *winter*

冬 冬 冬 冬 冬

xià   *summer*

夏　夏　夏　夏　夏　夏　夏　夏

rè   *hot*

熱　热　熱　熱　熱　熱　熱　熱　熱　熱

热　热　热　热　热　热

chūn   *spring*

春　春　春　春　春　春

qiū   *autumn; fall*

秋　秋　秋　秋

shū   *to smooth out*

舒

Characters from Proper Nouns

jiā   *to add*

加

zhōu   *administrative division*

州

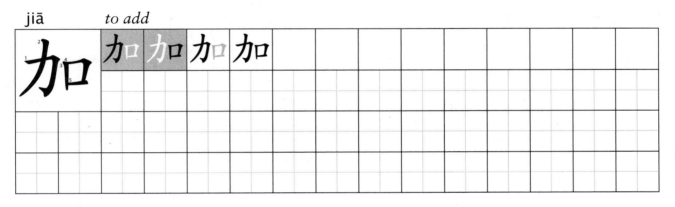

Dialogue I

xiàng   *likeness; portrait*

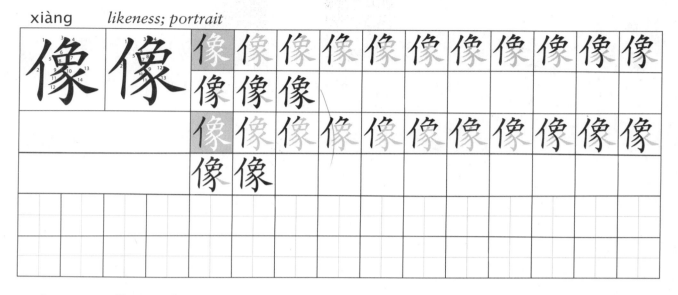

wù   *affair; task*

zhuō   *table*

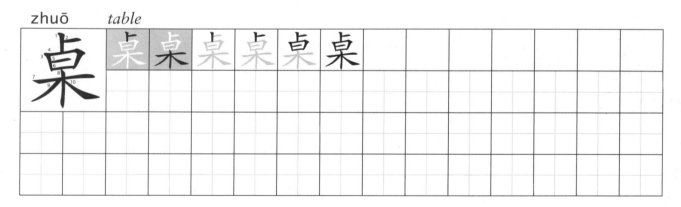

pán   *plate; dish*

盤 盘 | 盤 | 盤 | 盤 | 盤 | 盤 | 盤 | 盤 | 盤 | 盤 | 盤
盤 盤 盤
舟 盘 盘 盘 盘 盘 盘 盘 盘 盘
盘 盘

jiǎo   *dumpling*

餃 饺 | 餃 | 餃 | 餃 | 餃 | 餃
饺 | 饺 | 饺

sù   *vegetarian; made from vegetables*

素 | 素 | 素 | 素 | 素 | 素

dòu   *bean*

豆　豆 豆 豆 豆 豆 豆

fǔ   *rotten; turn bad*

腐　腐 腐 腐 腐 腐 腐

fàng   *to put; to place*

放　放 放 放 放

ròu   *meat*

肉　肉 肉 肉

wǎn — *bowl*

碗 碗 碗 碗 碗 碗 碗 碗 碗 碗 碗

suān — *sour*

酸 酸 酸 酸 酸 酸 酸 酸 酸 酸 酸 酸

là — *spicy; hot*

辣 辣 辣 辣 辣

tāng — *soup*

湯 汤 湯 湯 湯 湯 湯 湯 湯
汤 汤 汤 汤 汤

wèi   *flavor; taste*

味　味味味味

jīng   *essence; refined*

精　精精精精精精精

yán   *salt*

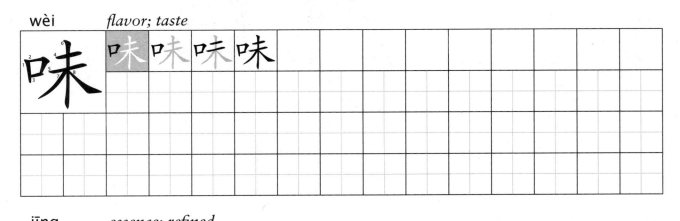

鹽　鹽鹽鹽鹽鹽鹽鹽鹽鹽鹽
盐　鹽鹽鹽鹽鹽鹽鹽鹽鹽鹽
　　盐盐盐盐

mài   *to sell*

賣　卖　賣　賣　賣　賣　賣
　　　　卖　卖　卖　卖

wán   *finished*

完　完　完　完

qīng   *blue; green*

青　青　青　青

kě   *thirsty*

渴　渴　渴　渴　渴　渴

xiē *(measure word for an indefinite amount); some*

些　些 些 些 些 些

gòu *enough*

夠 够　夠 夠 夠 夠 夠
　　　够 够 够 够 够

è *hungry*

餓 饿　餓 餓 餓
　　　饿 饿 饿

Dialogue II

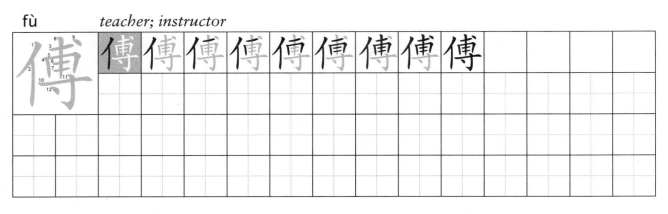

fù   *teacher; instructor*

傅 傅 傅 傅 傅 傅 傅 傅 傅

táng   *sugar*

糖 糖 糖 糖 糖 糖 糖 糖

cù   *vinegar*

醋 醋 醋 醋

yú   *fish*

魚 鱼 魚 魚 魚 魚
         鱼 鱼 鱼 鱼 鱼

tián   *sweet*

甜 甜 甜 甜 甜 甜 甜

jí   *extremely*

極 极 極 極 極 極 極 極
极 极 极

shāo   *to burn*

燒 烧 燒 燒 燒 燒 燒 燒 燒
烧 烧 烧 烧 烧 烧 烧 烧

niú   *cow; ox*

牛 牛 牛 牛 牛 牛

liáng   *cool*

涼 涼 涼 涼 涼 涼 涼 涼

bàn   *to mix*

拌 拌 拌 拌

guā   *melon; gourd*

瓜 瓜 瓜 瓜 瓜 瓜

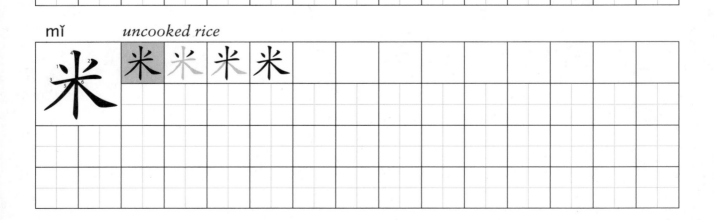

mǐ   *uncooked rice*

米 米 米 米 米

wàng   *to forget*

忘　忘 忘 忘

dài   *to bring; to take; to carry; to come with*

带 带　带 带 带 带 带 带 带 带
　　　带 带 带 带 带 带 带 带

qīng   *pure; clear*

清　清 清 清

chǔ   *neat*

楚　楚 楚 楚 楚 楚 楚 楚 楚 楚

guān   *to involve; to close*

關 关 闗 闗 闗 闗 關 關 關 關 關
关 关 关

xì   *to relate to*

係 系 係 係 係 係
系 系 系 系

yùn   *to move*

運   运   運 運 運 運 / 运 运 运 运 运

dòng   *to move*

動   动   動 動 動 / 动 动 动 动

páng   *side; edge*

旁   旁 旁 旁 旁 旁 旁

yuǎn   *far*

遠   远   遠 遠 遠 / 远 远 远

lí   *away from*

離 离 離 離 離 離 離 離 離 離
离 离 离 离 离 离 离 离

huó   *to live; living*

活 活 活 活

Dialogue II

ná *to take; to get*

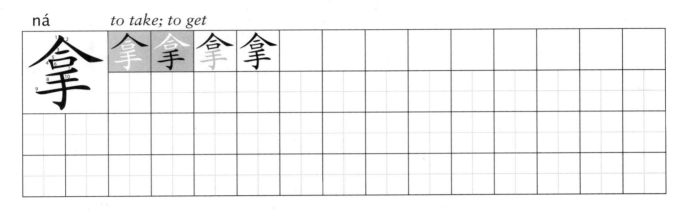

cì *(measure word for frequency)*

cóng *from*

zhí *straight*

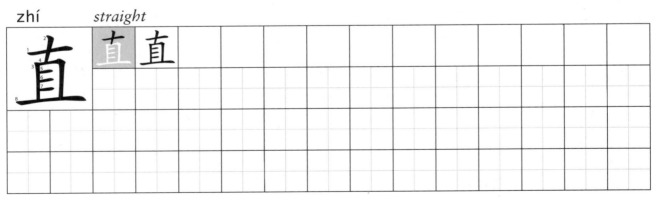

wǎng   *towards*

往 往 往 往 往

nán   *south*

南 南 南 南 南 南

guǎi   *to turn*

拐 拐 拐 拐

āi   *(exclamatory particle to express surprise or dissatisfaction)*

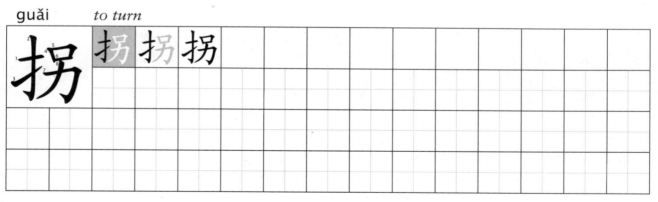

哎 哎 哎 哎 哎 哎
哎 哎 哎 哎 哎

dēng   *light*

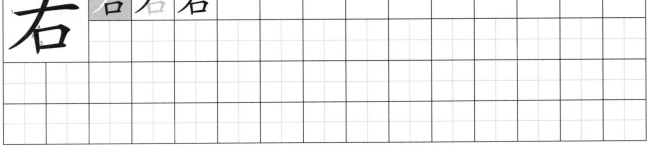

yòu   *right*

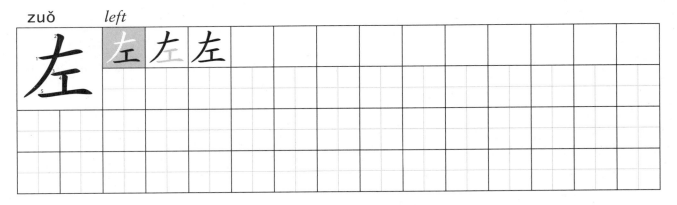

zuǒ   *left*

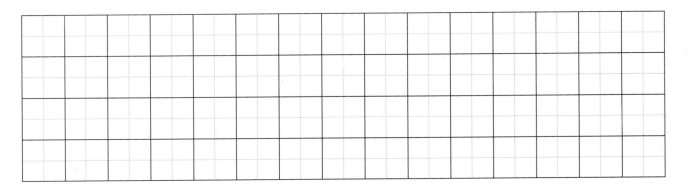

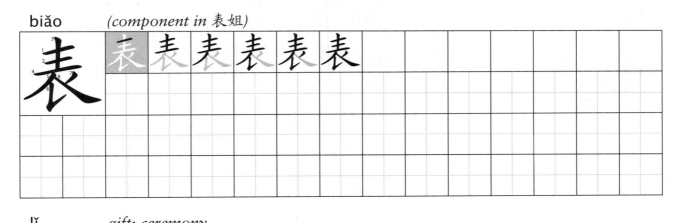

biǎo   *(component in* 表姐*)*

表

lǐ   *gift; ceremony*

禮 礼

wù   *thing; matter*

物

běn   *(measure word for books)*

本

yǐn   *to drink*

料   liào   *material*

bǎ   *(measure word for bunches of things, and chairs)*

píng   *(component in 蘋果/苹果)*

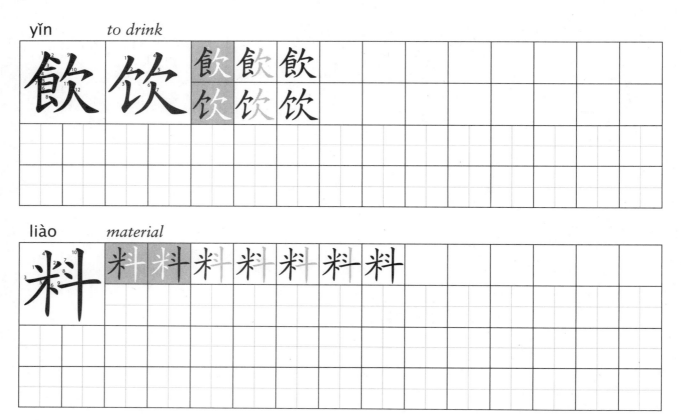

lí   *pear*

zhù   *to live (in a certain place)*

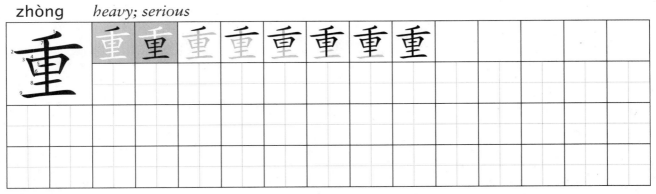

zhòng   *heavy; serious*

jiē   *to receive; to welcome, to go meet*

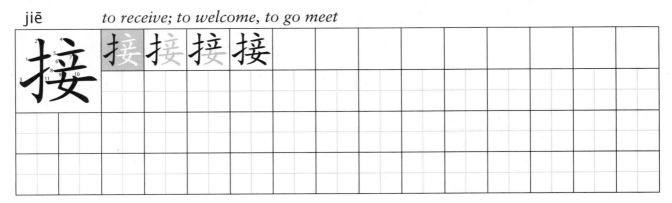

lóu   *multi-storied building; floor (of a multi-level building)*

楼 樓 樓 樓 樓 樓 樓 樓 樓
楼 楼 楼 楼

Dialogue II

zhōng   *clock*

鐘	钟	鐘 钟	鐘 钟	鐘 钟	鐘 钟					

tóu   *head*

頭	头	頭 头	頭 头	頭 头						
				头	头	头				

cōng   *able to hear well*

聰	聪	聰 聪	聰 聪	聰 聪	聰 聪	聰 聪	聰 聪	聰		

shǔ   *heat*

暑	暑	暑	暑							

bān   *class*

班   班 班 班 班 班

shǔ   *to belong to*

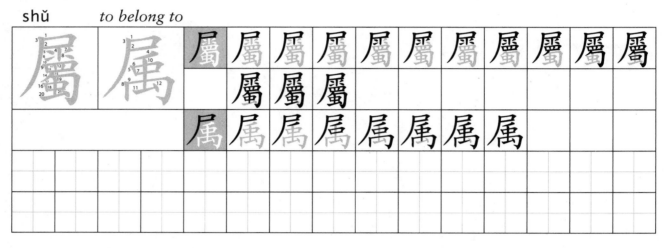

gǒu   *dog*

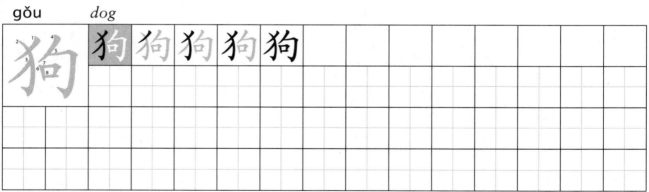

liǎn *face*

臉 脸 臉 臉 臉 臉 臉 臉 臉 臉
脸 脸 脸 脸 脸 脸 脸 脸

yuán *round*

圓 圆 圓 圓 圓 圓 圓
圆 圆 圆 圆 圆

yǎn *eye*

眼 眼 眼 眼

jīng *eyeball*

睛 睛 睛 睛

bí   *nose*

鼻 鼻 鼻 鼻 鼻 鼻 鼻

zuǐ   *mouth*

嘴 嘴 嘴 嘴 嘴 嘴 嘴 嘴

dìng   *settled; decided*

定 定 定 定 定 定 定

dàn   *egg*

蛋 蛋 蛋 蛋 蛋 蛋 蛋 蛋 蛋 蛋

Characters from Proper Nouns

lún   *ethics; moral principles*

mǔ   *housemaid*

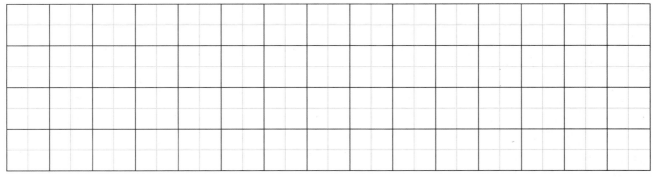

Dialogue I

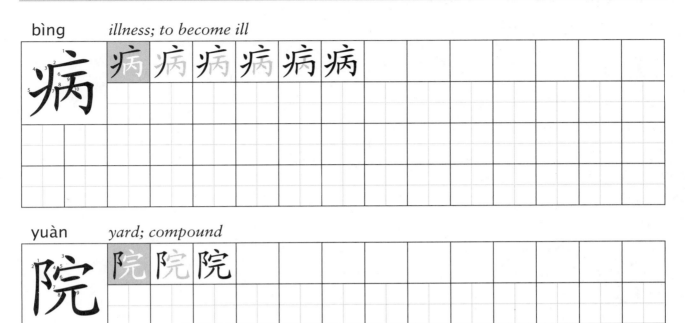

bìng   *illness; to become ill*

病

yuàn   *yard; compound*

院

dù   *belly; abdomen*

肚

téng   *to be painful*

疼

sǐ   *to die; (a complement indicating an extreme degree)*

yè   *night*

cè   *toilet*

xiāng   *box; case*

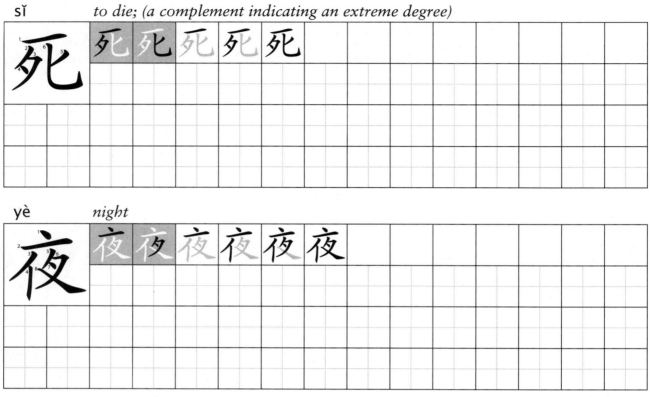

tǎng *to lie*

躺 躺 躺 躺 躺 躺 躺 躺 躺 躺 躺 躺

jiǎn *to inspect*

檢 檢 檢 檢 檢
检 检 检

chá *to look up*

查 查 查 查 查

huài *bad*

壞 坏 壞 壞 壞 壞 壞 壞 壞 壞 壞
坏 坏 坏

zhēn   *needle*

針 针 針 針 針
针 针 针

yào   *medicine*

藥 药 藥 藥 藥
药 药 药 药

piàn   *(measure word for tablet; slice)*

片 片 片 片 片 片

biàn   *(measure word for complete courses of an action or instances of an action)*

遍 遍 遍 遍

Dialogue II

gǎn   *to feel; to sense*

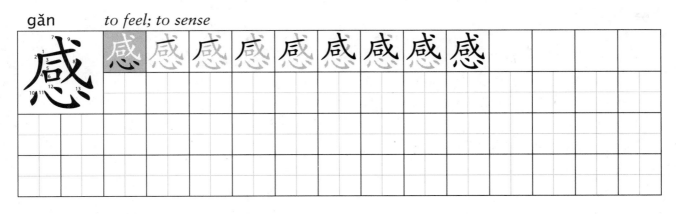

mào   *to belch; to emit*

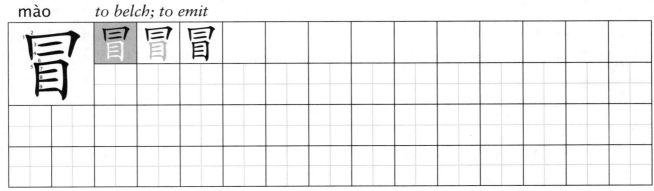

shēn   *body*

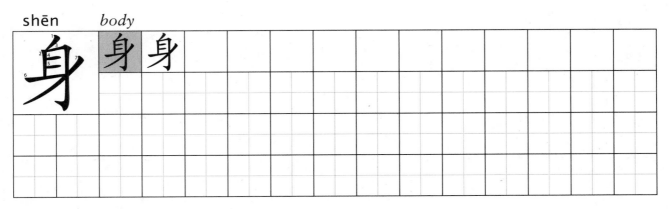

tǐ   *body*

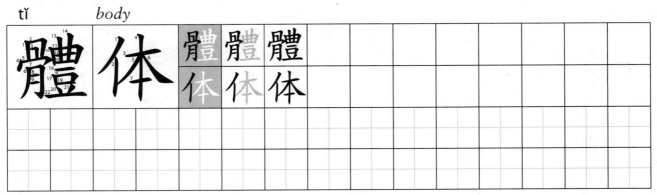

yǎng   *itchy*

癢   痒   癢 癢 癢 癢 癢 癢 癢
        痒 痒 痒

mǐn   *nimble; agile*

敏   敏 敏 敏

jiàn   *healthy*

健   健 健 健 健 健 健 健 健

kāng   *healthy; affluent*

康   康 康 康 康 康 康 康 康

bǎo   *insurance*

保 保保保保

xiǎn   *risk; danger*

險 险 险 险 险 / 险 险 险

gǎn   *to rush for*

趕 赶 赶 赶 赶 赶 / 赶 赶 赶

yuè   *to exceed*

越 越 越 越 越 越 越 越

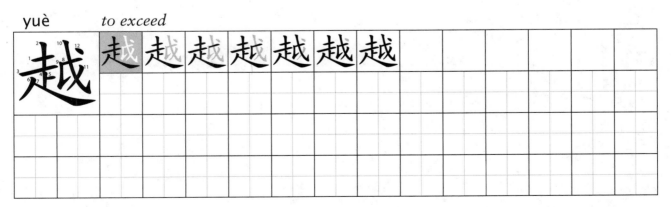

xiū   *to cease*

休　休休休

xī   *to cease*

息　息息息息

lǎn   *lazy*

懶　懶　懶懶懶懶懶懶懶
　　　　懶懶懶懶懶懶懶

luàn   *randomly; arbitrarily; messily*

亂乱　亂亂亂亂亂亂亂亂
　　　乱乱乱乱

Dialogue I

yìn   *to print*

印 印 印 印 印 印

xiàng   *appearance; shape*

象 象 象 象 象
象 象 象

chéng   *to become*

成 成 成 成 成 成 成

yǎn   *to show (a film); to perform*

演 演 演 演 演 演

fèi   *to spend; to take (effort)*

费   费   费   费   费   费   费   费
费   费   费

liǎ   *(coll.) two*

俩   俩   俩   俩   俩
俩   俩   俩

Dialogue II

jì   *to remember*

記 记 記 記 記
　　　　记 记 记

mǎ   *symbol indicating a number*

碼 码 碼 碼 碼
　　　　码 码 码

bān   *to move*

搬 搬 搬 搬 搬

sǎo   *to sweep*

掃 扫 掃 掃 掃 掃 掃 掃
　　　　扫 扫 扫

zhěng   *to put in order*

整　整 整 整 整 整

lǐ   *reason; in good order*

理　理 理 理

fáng   *house*

房　房 房 房 房

lǚ   *to travel*

旅　旅 旅 旅 旅 旅 旅 旅

Narrative

chǎo　　　*to quarrel; noisy*

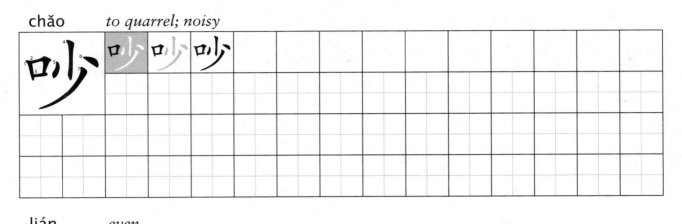

lián　　　*even*

guǎng　　　*wide; vast*

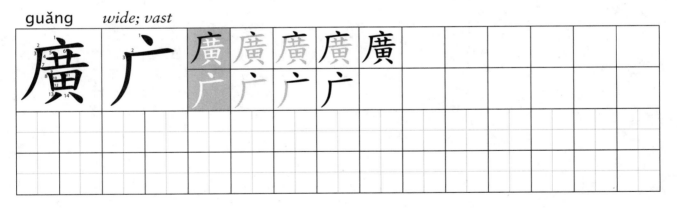

fù　　　*to attach; near*

tào   *(measure word for suite or set)*

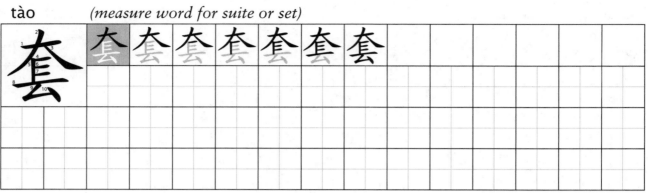

yù   *dwelling; residence*

wò   *to lie (down)*

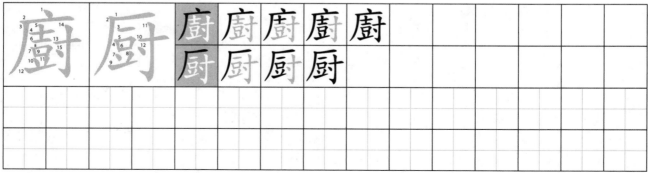

chú   *kitchen*

wèi   *to guard; to protect*

jiā   傢: *furniture;* 家: *family; home*

jù   *tool; utensil*

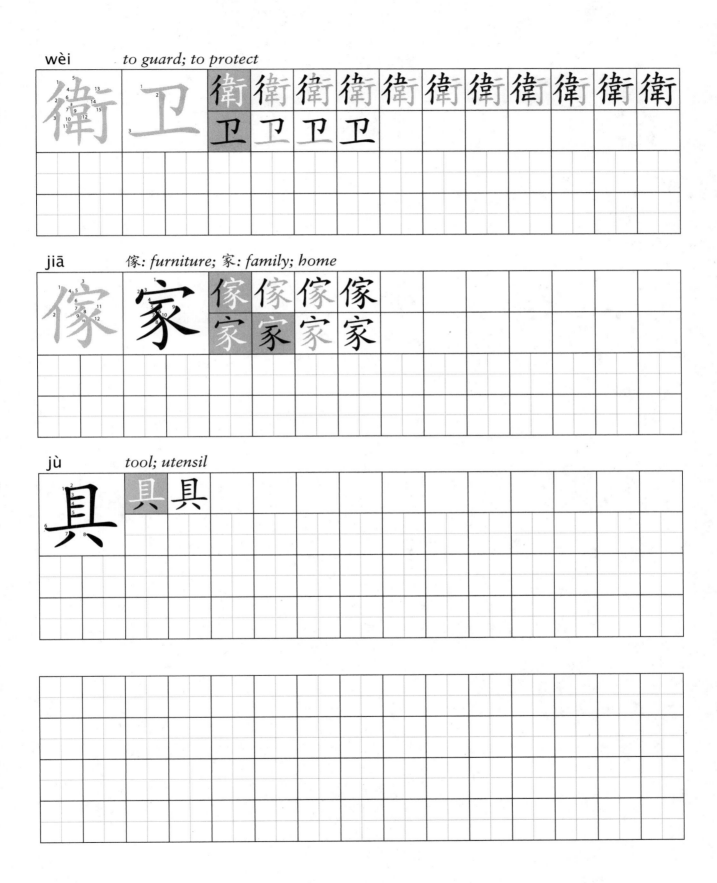

Dialogue

gān   *dry*

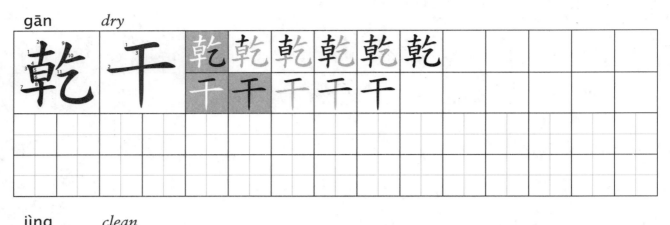

jìng   *clean*

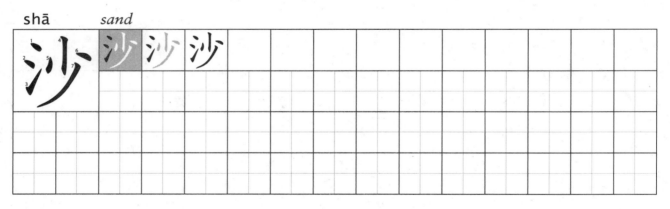

shā   *sand*

yǐ   *chair*

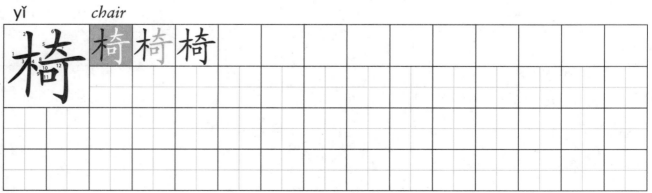

jià   *shelf*

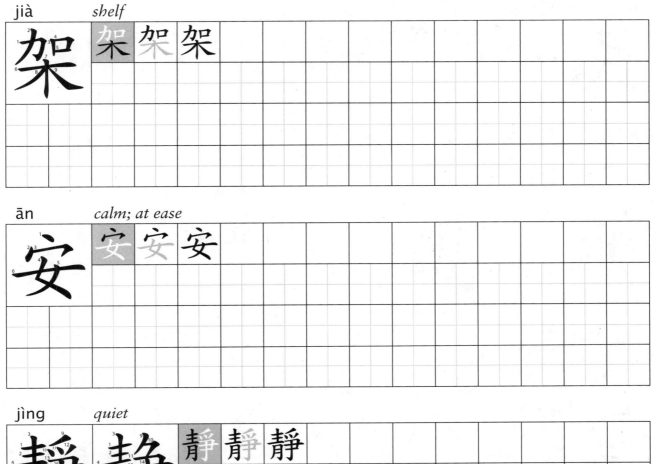

ān   *calm; at ease*

jìng   *quiet*

yuán   *(measure word for unit of Chinese currency); yuan*

mín   *the people*

民　民 民 民 民 民 民

bì   *currency*

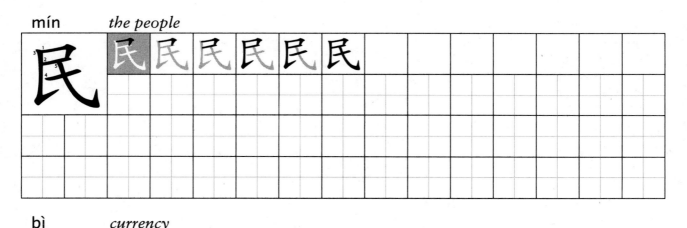

幣 幣 幣 幣 幣 幣 幣
巾 巾 巾 巾 巾

chà   *to fall short of*

差　差 差 差 差 差 差 差

yā   *to give as security*

押 押 押 押

dāng   *to serve as; to be*

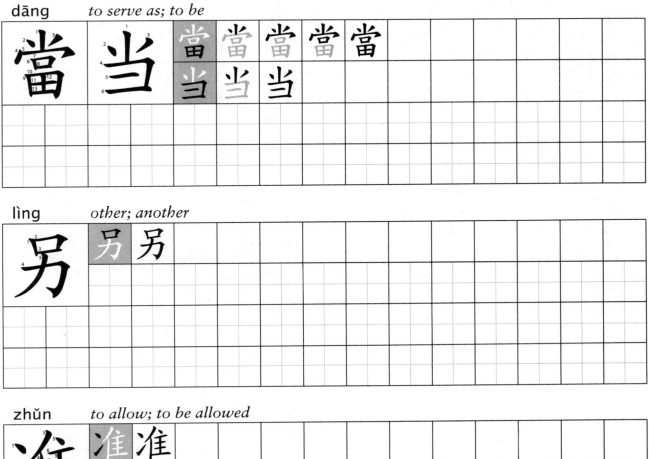

lìng   *other; another*

zhǔn   *to allow; to be allowed*

yǎng   *to raise*

qù   *interest; delight; aspiration*

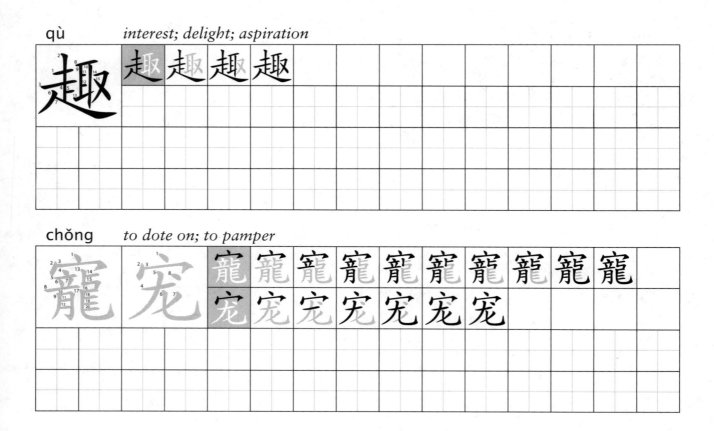

chǒng   *to dote on; to pamper*

Dialogue I

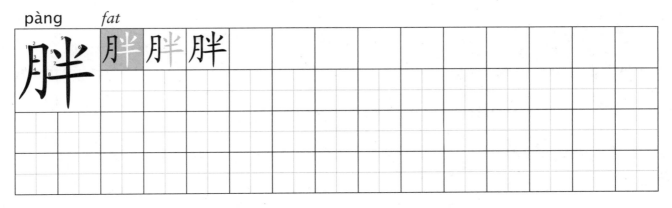

pàng *fat*

胖　胖　胖　胖

pà *to fear; to be afraid of*

怕　怕　怕　怕

jiǎn *simple*

簡　简　簡　簡　簡
　　　　简　简　简

dān *single*

單　单　單　單　單　單
　　　单　单　单　单

pǎo   *to run*

跑   跑 跑 跑 跑 跑 跑 跑

bù   *step; pace*

步   步 步 步 步 步

shòu   *to bear*

受   受 受 受 受 受

pāi   *racket*

拍   拍 拍 拍

lán   *basket*

籃 籃 籃 籃 籃
籃 籃

yóu   *to swim; to rove around*

游 游 游 游 游 游

yǒng   *swimming*

泳 泳 泳 泳 泳 泳 泳

wēi   *danger*

危 危 危 危 危 危

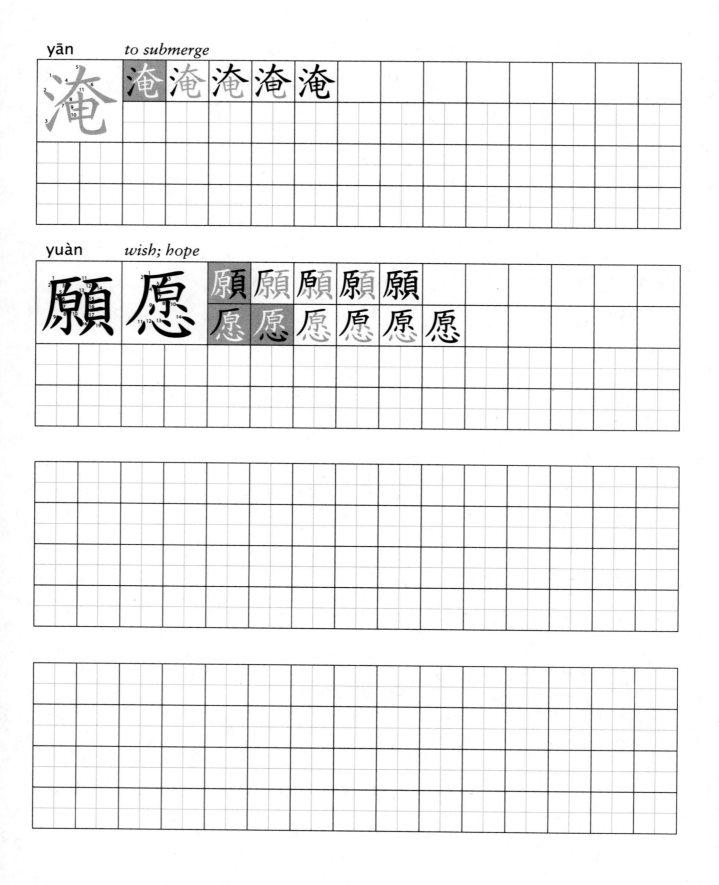

yān   *to submerge*

yuàn   *wish; hope*

Dialogue II

tí   *to lift*

提　提 提 提

sài   *game; match; competition*

賽　賽　賽 賽 賽 賽 賽 賽
賽 貝　賽 賽 賽 賽 賽

jì   *border; boundary*

際 际　際 際 際 際 際 際 際 際
际 际 际

shì   *type; style*

式　式 式 式 式

yīng   *should; ought to*

應 应 應 應 應 應 雁 應
应 应 应 应 应 应

gāi   *should; ought to*

該 该 該 該 該 該 該 該 該
该 该 该 该 该 该 该 该

jiǎo   *foot*

tī   *to kick*

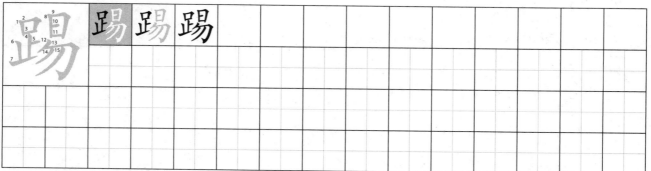

bào   *to hold or carry in the arms*

抱   抱 抱 抱

yā   *to press; to hold down; to weigh down*

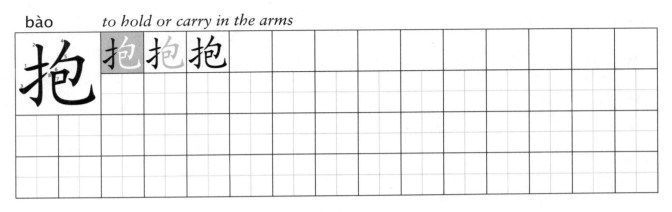

bèi   *by*

被   被 被 被 被 被 被

dān   *to be burdened with*

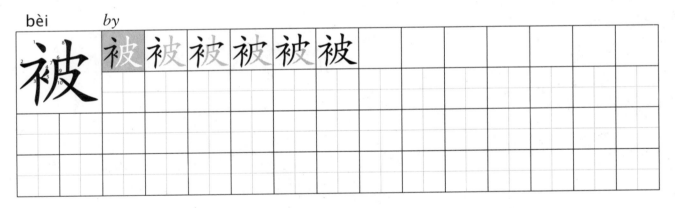

bàng   *fantastic*

棒 棒 棒 棒 棒 棒

Dialogue I

sī   *to take charge of*

司   司 司 司 司 司

shí   *solid; reality*

實 实 實 實 實 實 實 實 實
              实 实 实

jì   *to count; idea*

計 计 計 計 計
           计 计 计

huà   *plan*

劃 划 劃 劃 劃 劃 劃
           划 划 划 划 划 划 划

fù   *father*

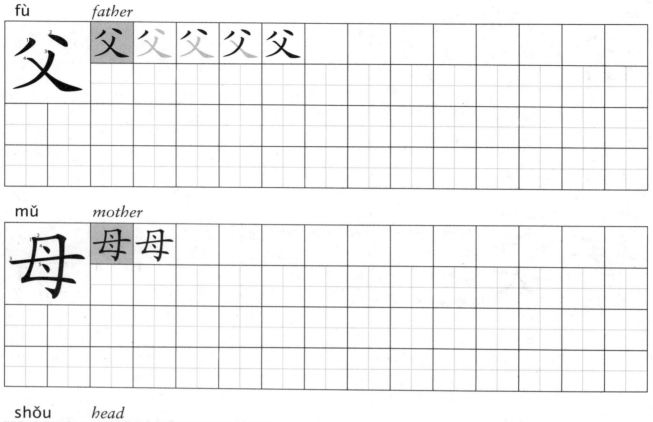

mǔ   *mother*

shǒu   *head*

zhèng   *politics*

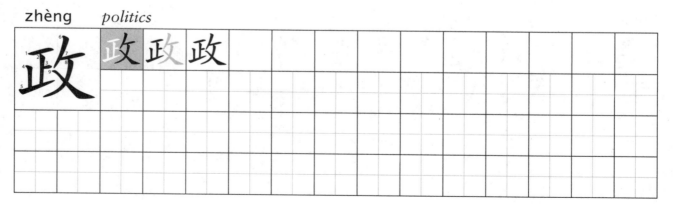

zhì *to govern; to manage*

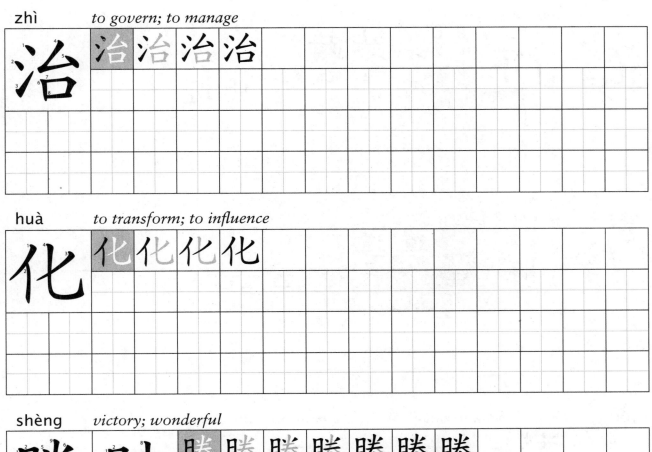

huà *to transform; to influence*

shèng *victory; wonderful*

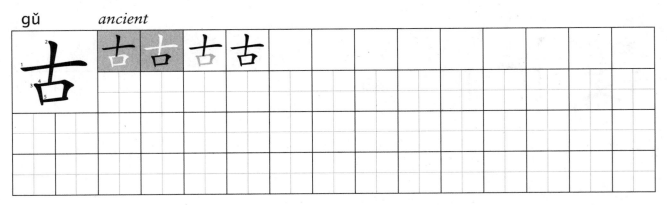

gǔ *ancient*

jì   *remains; ruins*

蹟 迹 蹟 蹟 蹟 蹟
迹 迹 迹 迹 迹 迹 迹

dǎo   *to lead; to guide*

導 导 導 導 導
寸 导 导 导 导 导

yóu   遊：*to roam; to travel;* 游：*to swim; to rove around*

遊 游 遊 遊 遊 遊 遊
游 游

hù   *to protect*

護 护 護 護 護 護 護 護
护 护 护

dìng   *to reserve; to book (a ticket, a hotel room, etc.)*

訂　订

qiān   *to sign*

簽　签

zhèng   *proof; certificate*

證　证

shè   *organized body*

社

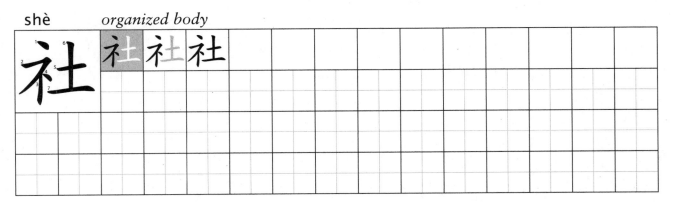

Characters from Proper Nouns

xiāng   *fragrant*

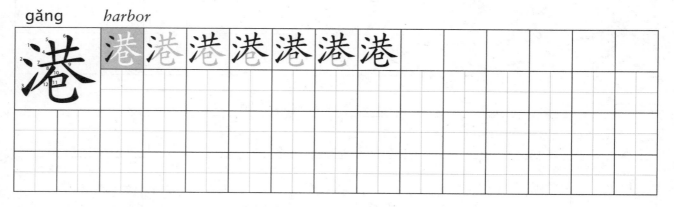

gǎng   *harbor*

tái   *platform; deck*

Dialogue II

chū *beginning*

初　初 初 初 初

chéng *journey*

程　程 程 程 程

fǎn *to return*

返　返 返 返

háng *to navigate*

航　航 航 航 航

qiān   *thousand*

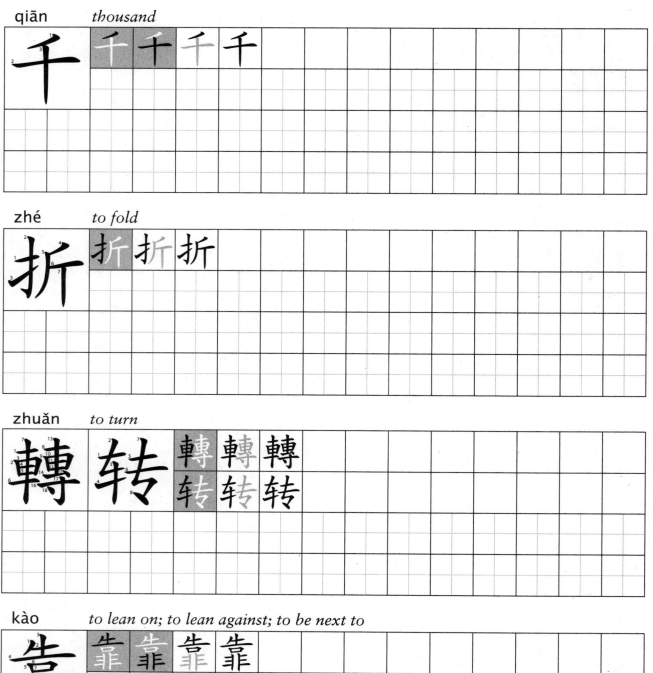

zhé   *to fold*

zhuǎn   *to turn*

kào   *to lean on; to lean against; to be next to*

chuāng   *window*

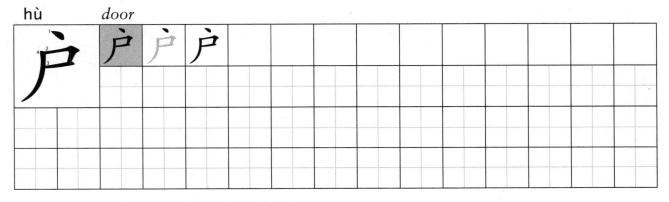

hù   *door*

戸

份

fèn   *(measure word for meal order, job)*

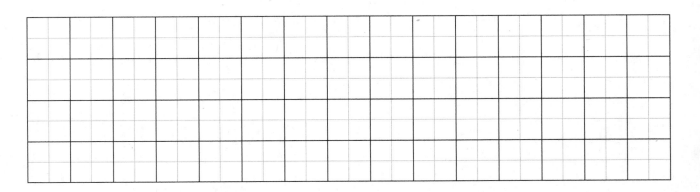

Dialogue I

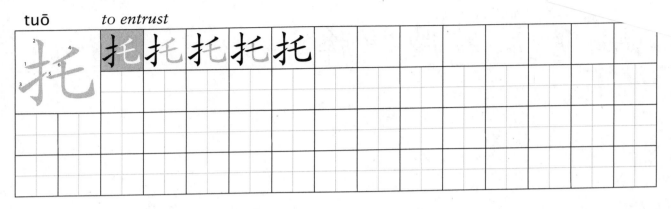

tuō   *to entrust*

托 托 托 托 托 托

bāo   *bag; sack; bundle; package*

包 包 包 包

chāo   *to exceed; to surpass*

超 超 超 超 超

dēng   *to climb; to ascend*

登 登 登 登

pái   *plate; tablet; card*

牌 牌 牌 牌 牌 牌 牌

kū   *to cry; to weep*

哭 哭 哭 哭 哭 哭 哭

gù   *to look after; to attend to*

顧 顾 顧 顧 顧

顧 顾 顾 顾 顾 顾

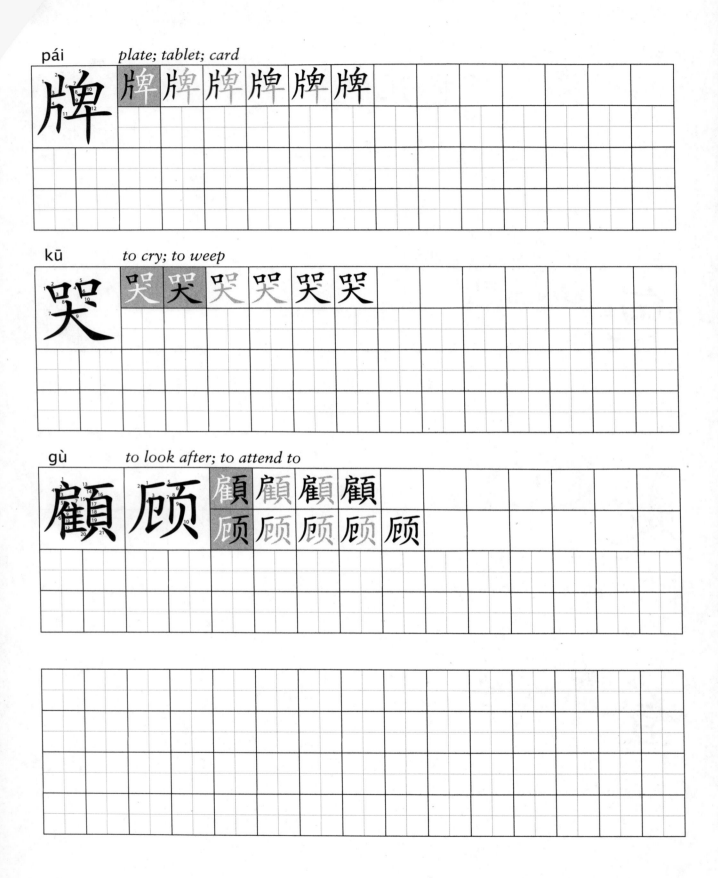

Dialogue II

shū   *uncle*

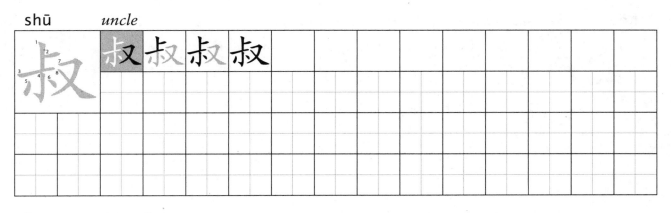

ā   *(a prefix)*

yí   *aunt*

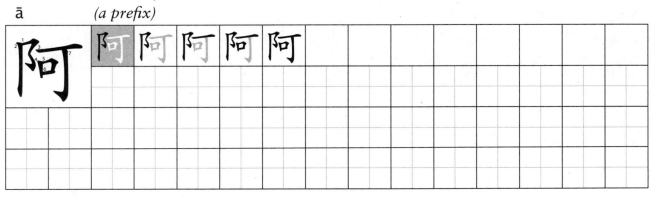

yíng   *to welcome*

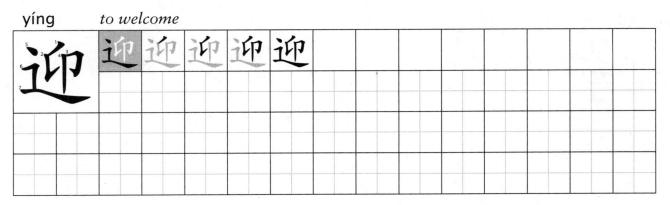

shòu   *thin, slim (usually of a person or animal); lean*

瘦 瘦 瘦 瘦 瘦 瘦 瘦 瘦 瘦 瘦

yé   *(respectful form of address for an elderly man)*

爺 爺 爺 爺
爷 爷 爷 爷

nǎi   *milk*

奶 奶 奶 奶

kǎo   *to bake; to roast; to grill*

烤 烤 烤

yā　　　*duck*

鴨　鴨　鴨 鴨 鴨 鴨 鴨 鴨 鴨 鴨 鴨 鴨 鴨
　　　鴨 鴨 鴨 鴨 鴨 鴨 鴨

INDEX A
Characters Alphabetically by Pinyin

P = pinyin
T = traditional form
S = simplified form
L = lesson

Pinyin	Traditional	Simplified	Meaning	Ch	Pg
ér	而		(conj.)	11	3
fǎn	返		to return	19	71
fáng	房		house	16	48
fàng	放		to put; to place	12	11
fēi	非		not, non-	11	5
fèi	費	费	to spend; to take (effort)	16	46
fèn	份		(measure word for meal order, job)	19	73
fǔ	腐		rotten; turn bad	12	11
fù	傅		teacher; instructor	12	16
fù	附		to attach; near	17	49
fù	父		father	19	66
gāi	該	该	should; ought to	18	62
gān	乾	干	dry	17	52
gǎn	感		to feel; to sense	15	41
gǎn	趕	赶	to rush for	15	43
gāng	剛	刚	just now	11	2
gǎng	港		harbor	19	70
gāo	糕		cake	11	5
gèng	更		even more	11	2
gǒu	狗		dog	14	32
gòu	夠	够	enough	12	15
gǔ	古		ancient	19	67
gù	顧	顾	to look after; to attend to	20	76
guā	瓜		melon; gourd	12	18
guǎi	拐		to turn	13	24
guān	關	关	to involve; to close	12	20
guǎng	廣	广	wide; vast	17	49
háng	航		to navigate	19	71
hù	護	护	to protect	19	68
hù	戶		door	19	73
huá	滑		slippery; to slide	11	1
huà	劃	划	plan	19	65
huà	化		to transform; to influence	19	67
huài	壞	坏	bad	15	39
huó	活		to live; living	13	22
jí	極	极	extremely	12	17
jì	記	记	to remember	16	47
jì	際	际	border; boundary	18	61
jì	計	计	to count; idea	19	65
jì	蹟	迹	remains; ruins	19	68
jiā	加		to add	11	7
jiā	傢	家	傢: furniture; 家: family; home	17	51
jià	架		shelf	17	53
jiǎn	檢	检	to inspect	15	39
jiǎn	簡	简	simple	18	57
jiàn	健		healthy	15	42
jiǎo	餃	饺	dumpling	12	10
jiǎo	腳	脚	foot	18	62
jiē	接		to receive; to welcome, to go meet	14	29
jīng	精		essence; refined	12	13
jīng	睛		eyeball	14	33
jìng	淨	净	clean	17	52
jìng	靜	静	quiet	17	53
jù	具		tool; utensil	17	51
kāng	康		healthy; affluent	15	42
kǎo	烤		to bake; to roast; to grill	20	78
kào	靠		to lean on; to lean against; to be next to	19	72
kě	渴		thirsty	12	14
kū	哭		to cry; to weep	20	76
là	辣		spicy; hot	12	12
lán	籃	篮	basket	18	59
lǎn	懶	懒	lazy	15	44
lěng	冷		cold	11	3
lí	離	离	away from	13	22
lí	梨		pear	14	29
lǐ	禮	礼	gift; ceremony	14	27
lǐ	理		reason; in good order	16	48
liǎ	倆	俩	(coll.) two	16	46
lián	連	连	even	17	49
liǎn	臉	脸	face	14	33
liáng	涼	凉	cool	12	18

liào	料		material	14	28
lìng	另		other; another	17	55
lóu	樓	楼	multi-storied building; floor (of a multi-level building)	14	30
lǚ	旅		to travel	16	48
luàn	亂	乱	randomly; arbitrarily; messily	15	44
lún	倫	伦	ethics; moral principles	14	35
mǎ	碼	码	symbol indicating a number	16	47
mài	賣	卖	to sell	12	14
mào	冒		to belch; to emit	15	41
mǐ	米		uncooked rice	12	18
mín	民		the people	17	54
mǐn	敏		nimble; agile	15	42
mǔ	姆		housemaid	14	35
mǔ	母		mother	19	66
ná	拿		to take; to get	13	23
nǎi	奶		milk	20	78
nán	南		south	13	24
niú	牛		cow; ox	12	17
nuǎn	暖		warm	11	3
pà	怕		to fear; to be afraid of	18	57
pāi	拍		racket	18	58
pái	牌		plate; tablet; card	20	76
pán	盤	盘	plate; dish	12	10
páng	旁		side; edge	13	21
pàng	胖		fat	18	57
pǎo	跑		to run	18	58
piàn	片		(measure word for tablet; slice)	15	40
píng	蘋	苹	(component in 蘋果/苹果)	14	28
qiān	簽	签	to sign	19	69
qiān	千		thousand	19	72
qiě	且		(conj.)	11	3
qīng	青		blue; green	12	14
qīng	清		pure; clear	12	19
qiū	秋		autumn; fall	11	6
qù	趣		interest; delight; aspiration	17	56
rè	熱	热	hot	11	6
ròu	肉		meat	12	11
sài	賽	赛	game; match; competition	18	61
sǎo	掃	扫	to sweep	16	47
shā	沙		sand	17	52
shāo	燒	烧	to burn	12	17
shè	社		organized body	19	69
shēn	身		body	15	41
shèng	勝	胜	victory; wonderful	19	67
shí	實	实	solid; reality	19	65
shì	式		type; style	18	61
shǒu	首		head	19	66
shòu	受		to bear	18	58
shòu	瘦		thin, slim (usually of a person or animal); lean	20	78
shū	舒		to smooth out	11	7
shū	叔		uncle	20	77
shǔ	暑		heat	14	31
shǔ	屬	属	to belong to	14	32
sī	司		to take charge of	19	65
sǐ	死		to die; (a complement indicating an extreme degree)	15	38
sù	素		vegetarian; made from vegetables	12	10
suān	酸		sour	12	12
tái	台		platform; deck	19	70
tāng	湯	汤	soup	12	12
táng	糖		sugar	12	16
tǎng	躺		to lie	15	39
tào	套		(measure word for suite or set)	17	50
téng	疼		to be painful	15	37
tī	踢		to kick	18	62

zhōng	鐘	钟	clock	14	31
zhòng	重		heavy; serious	14	29
zhōu	州		administrative division	11	7
zhù	住		to live (in a certain place)	14	29
zhuǎn	轉	转	to turn	19	72
zhǔn	准		to allow; to be allowed	17	55
zhuō	桌		table	12	9
zuǐ	嘴		mouth	14	34
zuǒ	左		left	13	25

INDEX B
Characters by Lesson and by Pinyin

P = pinyin
T = traditional form
S = simplified form
L = lesson

P	T	S	Definition	L	Page
bào	報	报	newspaper; to report	11	2
bǐ	比		to compare	11	1
bīng	冰		ice	11	2
chūn	春		spring	11	6
dié	碟		disc; small plate, dish, saucer	11	4
dōng	冬		winter	11	5
ér	而		(conj.)	11	3
fēi	非		not, non–	11	5
gāng	剛	刚	just now	11	2
gāo	糕		cake	11	5
gèng	更		even more	11	2
huá	滑		slippery; to slide	11	1
jiā	加		to add	11	7
lěng	冷		cold	11	3
nuǎn	暖		warm	11	3
qiě	且		(conj.)	11	3
qiū	秋		autumn; fall	11	6
rè	熱	热	hot	11	6
shū	舒		to smooth out	11	7
xià	夏		summer	11	6
xuě	雪		snow	11	1
yuán	園	园	garden	11	1
zāo	糟		rotten, decayed	11	5
zhōu	州		administrative division	11	7
bàn	拌		to mix	12	18
chǔ	楚		neat	12	19
cù	醋		vinegar	12	16
dài	帶	带	to bring; to take; to carry; to come with	12	19
dòu	豆		bean	12	11
è	餓	饿	hungry	12	15
fàng	放		to put; to place	12	11
fǔ	腐		rotten; turn bad	12	11
fù	傅		teacher; instructor	12	16
gòu	夠	够	enough	12	15
guā	瓜		melon; gourd	12	18
guān	關	关	to involve; to close	12	20
jí	極	极	extremely	12	17
jiǎo	餃	饺	dumpling	12	10
jīng	精		essence; refined	12	13
kě	渴		thirsty	12	14
là	辣		spicy; hot	12	12
liáng	涼	凉	cool	12	18
mài	賣	卖	to sell	12	14
mǐ	米		uncooked rice	12	18
niú	牛		cow; ox	12	17
pán	盤	盘	plate; dish	12	10
qīng	青		blue; green	12	14
qīng	清		pure; clear	12	19
ròu	肉		meat	12	11
shāo	燒	烧	to burn	12	17
sù	素		vegetarian; made from vegetables	12	10
suān	酸		sour	12	12
tāng	湯	汤	soup	12	12
táng	糖		sugar	12	16
tián	甜		sweet	12	17
wán	完		finished	12	14
wǎn	碗		bowl	12	12
wàng	忘		to forget	12	19
wèi	味		flavor; taste	12	13
wù	務	务	affair; task	12	9
xì	係	系	to relate to	12	20
xiàng	像	像	likeness; portrait	12	9

xiē	些		(measure word for an indefinite amount); some	12	15
yán	鹽	盐	salt	12	13
yú	魚	鱼	fish	12	16
zhuō	桌		table	12	9
āi	哎	哎	(exclamatory particle to express surprise or dissatisfaction)	13	24
cì	次		(measure word for frequency)	13	23
cóng	從	从	from	13	23
dēng	燈	灯	light	13	25
dòng	動	动	to move	13	21
guǎi	拐		to turn	13	24
huó	活		to live; living	13	22
lí	離	离	away from	13	22
ná	拿		to take; to get	13	23
nán	南		south	13	24
páng	旁		side; edge	13	21
wǎng	往		towards	13	24
yòu	右		right	13	25
yuǎn	遠	远	far	13	21
yùn	運	运	to move	13	21
zhí	直		straight	13	23
zuǒ	左		left	13	25
bǎ	把		(measure word for bunches of things, and chairs)	14	28
bān	班		class	14	32
běn	本		(measure word for books)	14	27
bí	鼻		nose	14	34
biǎo	表		(component in 表姐)	14	27
cōng	聰	聪	able to hear well	14	31
dàn	蛋		egg	14	34
dìng	定		settled; decided	14	34
gǒu	狗		dog	14	32
jiē	接		to receive; to welcome, to go meet	14	29
jīng	睛		eyeball	14	33
lí	梨		pear	14	29
lǐ	禮	礼	gift; ceremony	14	27
liǎn	臉	脸	face	14	33
liào	料		material	14	28
lóu	樓	楼	multi-storied building; floor (of a multi-level building)	14	30
lún	倫	伦	ethics; moral principles	14	35
mǔ	姆		housemaid	14	35
píng	蘋	苹	(component in 蘋果/苹果)	14	28
shǔ	暑		heat	14	31
shǔ	屬	属	to belong to	14	32
tóu	頭	头	head	14	31
wù	物		thing; matter	14	27
yǎn	眼		eye	14	33
yǐn	飲	饮	to drink	14	28
yuán	圓	圆	round	14	33
zhōng	鐘	钟	clock	14	31
zhòng	重		heavy; serious	14	29
zhù	住		to live (in a certain place)	14	29
zuǐ	嘴		mouth	14	34
bǎo	保		insurance	15	43
biàn	遍		(measure word for complete courses of an action or instances of an action)	15	40
bìng	病		illness; to become ill	15	37
cè	廁	厕	toilet	15	38
chá	查		to look up	15	39
dù	肚		belly; abdomen	15	37
gǎn	感		to feel; to sense	15	41
gǎn	趕	赶	to rush for	15	43
huài	壞	坏	bad	15	39
jiǎn	檢	检	to inspect	15	39
jiàn	健		healthy	15	42
kāng	康		healthy; affluent	15	42

lǎn	懶	懒	lazy	15	44
luàn	亂	乱	randomly; arbitrarily; messily	15	44
mào	冒		to belch; to emit	15	41
mǐn	敏		nimble; agile	15	42
piàn	片		(measure word for tablet; slice)	15	40
shēn	身		body	15	41
sǐ	死		to die; (a complement indicating an extreme degree)	15	38
tǎng	躺		to lie	15	39
téng	疼		to be painful	15	37
tǐ	體	体	body	15	41
xī	息		to cease	15	44
xiǎn	險	险	risk; danger	15	43
xiāng	箱		box; case	15	38
xiū	休		to cease	15	44
yǎng	癢	痒	itchy	15	42
yào	藥	药	medicine	15	40
yè	夜		night	15	38
yuàn	院		yard; compound	15	37
yuè	越		to exceed	15	43
zhēn	針	针	needle	15	40
bān	搬		to move	16	47
chéng	成		to become	16	45
fáng	房		house	16	48
fèi	費	费	to spend; to take (effort)	16	46
jì	記	记	to remember	16	47
lǐ	理		reason; in good order	16	48
liǎ	倆	俩	(coll.) two	16	46
lǚ	旅		to travel	16	48
mǎ	碼	码	symbol indicating a number	16	47
sǎo	掃	扫	to sweep	16	47
xiàng	象	象	appearance; shape	16	45
yǎn	演		to show (a film); to perform	16	45
yìn	印		to print	16	45
zhěng	整		to put in order	16	48
ān	安		calm; at ease	17	53
bì	幣	币	currency	17	54
chà	差		to fall short of	17	54
chǎo	吵		to quarrel; noisy	17	49
chǒng	寵	宠	to dote on; to pamper	17	56
chú	廚	厨	kitchen	17	50
dāng	當	当	to serve as; to be	17	55
fù	附		to attach; near	17	49
gān	乾	干	dry	17	52
guǎng	廣	广	wide; vast	17	49
jiā	傢	家	傢: furniture; 家: family; home	17	51
jià	架		shelf	17	53
jìng	淨	净	clean	17	52
jìng	靜	静	quiet	17	53
jù	具		tool; utensil	17	51
lián	連	连	even	17	49
lìng	另		other; another	17	55
mín	民		the people	17	54
qù	趣		interest; delight; aspiration	17	56
shā	沙		sand	17	52
tào	套		(measure word for suite or set)	17	50
wèi	衛	卫	to guard; to protect	17	51
wò	臥	卧	to lie (down)	17	50
yā	押		to give as security	17	54
yǎng	養	养	to raise	17	55
yǐ	椅		chair	17	52
yù	寓		dwelling; residence	17	50
yuán	元		(measure word for unit of Chinese currency); yuan	17	53
zhǔn	准		to allow; to be allowed	17	55
bàng	棒		fantastic	18	64

Pinyin	Trad.	Simp.	Meaning		
bào	抱		to hold or carry in the arms	18	63
bèi	被		by	18	63
bù	步		step; pace	18	58
dān	單	单	single	18	57
dān	擔	担	to be burdened with	18	63
gāi	該	该	should; ought to	18	62
jì	際	际	border; boundary	18	61
jiǎn	簡	简	simple	18	57
jiǎo	腳	脚	foot	18	62
lán	籃	篮	basket	18	59
pà	怕		to fear; to be afraid of	18	57
pāi	拍		racket	18	58
pàng	胖		fat	18	57
pǎo	跑		to run	18	58
sài	賽	赛	game; match; competition	18	61
shì	式		type; style	18	61
shòu	受		to bear	18	58
tī	踢		to kick	18	62
tí	提		to lift	18	61
wēi	危		danger	18	59
yā	壓	压	to press; to hold down; to weigh down	18	63
yān	淹		to submerge	18	60
yīng	應	应	should; ought to	18	62
yǒng	泳		swimming	18	59
yóu	游		to swim; to rove around	18	59
yuàn	願	愿	wish; hope	18	60
chéng	程		journey	19	71
chū	初		beginning	19	71
chuāng	窗		window	19	73
dǎo	導	导	to lead; to guide	19	68
dìng	訂	订	to reserve; to book (a ticket, a hotel room, etc.)	19	69
fǎn	返		to return	19	71
fèn	份		(measure word for meal order, job)	19	73
fù	父		father	19	66
gǎng	港		harbor	19	70
gǔ	古		ancient	19	67
háng	航		to navigate	19	71
yóu	遊	游	遊:to roam; to travel; 游: to swim; to rove around	19	68
hù	護	护	to protect	19	68
hù	戶	户	door	19	73
huà	劃	划	plan	19	65
huà	化		to transform; to influence	19	67
jì	計	计	to count; idea	19	65
jì	蹟	迹	remains; ruins	19	68
kào	靠		to lean on; to lean against; to be next to	19	72
mǔ	母		mother	19	66
qiān	簽	签	to sign	19	69
qiān	千		thousand	19	72
shè	社		organized body	19	69
shèng	勝	胜	victory; wonderful	19	67
shí	實	实	solid; reality	19	65
shǒu	首		head	19	66
sī	司		to take charge of	19	65
tái	台		platform; deck	19	70
xiāng	香		fragrant	19	70
zhé	折		to fold	19	72
zhèng	政		politics	19	66
zhèng	證	证	proof; certificate	19	69
zhì	治		to govern; to manage	19	67
zhuǎn	轉	转	to turn	19	72
ā	阿		(a prefix)	20	77
bāo	包		bag; sack; bundle; package	20	75
chāo	超		to exceed; to surpass	20	75
dēng	登		to climb; to ascend	20	75

gù	顧	顾	to look after; to attend to	20	76
kǎo	烤		to bake; to roast; to grill	20	78
kū	哭		to cry; to weep	20	
76nǎi	奶		milk	20	78
pái	牌		plate; tablet; card	20	76
shòu	瘦		thin, slim (usually of a person or animal); lean	20	78
shū	叔		uncle	20	77
tuō	托		to entrust	20	75
yā	鴨	鸭	duck	20	79
yé	爺	爷	(respectful form of address for an elderly man)	20	78
yí	姨		aunt	20	77
yíng	迎		to welcome	20	77

Expand your *Integrated Chinese* Study

with support for the whole series

Textbooks, Workbooks, Character Workbooks, Teacher's Handbooks, and **Audio CDs** *work together as a comprehensive curriculum.*

Online Workbooks, eTextbooks, BuilderCards, and **Textbook DVDs for all levels** *take study further and add flexibility to the classroom.*

INTEGRATED CHINESE COMPANION WEBSITE
More supplements for students, more support for teachers!

www.cheng-tsui.com/integratedchinese

Kù Chinese

eFlashcards

STUDENTS Sharpen your vocabulary recognition and pronunciation with new *eFlashcards* and learn fun idioms and slang with the video series *Kù Chinese*.

TEACHERS Enhance your classroom instruction with *Video Activity Worksheets* (available for all *Integrated Chinese* DVDs), sentence pattern drills, teacher-generated PowerPoints®, and additional tools for testing and assessment.

Visit **www.cheng-tsui.com** or call 1-800-554-1963 for more information about other supplementary materials, such as graded readers, listening comprehension workbooks, character guides, and reference materials.